LO[illegible] POEMS ON THE UNDERGROUND

edited by

Gerard Benson

Judith Chernaik

Cicely Herbert

Cassell Publishers Limited
Wellington House, 125 Strand
London WC2R 0BB

First published 1996

British Library Cataloguing in Publication Data
A catalogue record for this book is available from the British Library

ISBN 0–304–34902–X

Cover illustration by Annabel Wilson

Typeset in Monotype Meridien by
KDI, Newton le Willows, Lancs.

Printed and bound in Great Britain by
Hillman Printers Ltd

CONTENTS

THE POEMS

Like a Beacon

In London
every now and then
I get this craving
for my mother's food
I leave art galleries
in search of plantains
saltfish/sweet potatoes

I need this link

I need this touch
of home
swinging my bag
like a beacon
against the cold

GRACE NICHOLS (b. 1950)

At Lord's

It is little I repair to the matches of the Southron folk,
  Though my own red roses there may blow;
It is little I repair to the matches of the Southron folk,
  Though the red roses crest the caps, I know.
For the field is full of shades as I near the shadowy coast,
And a ghostly batsman plays to the bowling of a ghost,
And I look through my tears on a soundless-clapping host
  As the run-stealers flicker to and fro,
      To and fro: –
  O my Hornby and my Barlow long ago!

FRANCIS THOMPSON (1859–1907)

Encounter at St. Martin's

I tell a wanderer's tale, the same
I began long ago, a boy in a barn,
I am always lost in it. The place
is always strange to me. In my pocket

the wrong money or none, the wrong paper,
maps of another town, the phrase book
for yesterday's language, just a ticket
to the next station, and my instructions.

In the lobby of the Banco Bilbao
a dark woman will slip me a key, a package,
the name of a hotel, a numbered account,
the first letters of an unknown alphabet.

KEN SMITH (b. 1938)

Composed upon Westminster Bridge, September 3, 1802

Earth has not anything to show more fair:
Dull would he be of soul who could pass by
A sight so touching in its majesty:
This City now doth like a garment wear
The beauty of the morning; silent, bare,
Ships, towers, domes, theatres, and temples lie
Open unto the fields, and to the sky;
All bright and glittering in the smokeless air.
Never did sun more beautifully steep
In his first splendour valley, rock, or hill;
Ne'er saw I, never felt, a calm so deep!
The river glideth at his own sweet will:
Dear God! the very houses seem asleep;
And all that mighty heart is lying still!

WILLIAM WORDSWORTH (1770–1850)

Immigrant

November '63: eight months in London.
I pause on the low bridge to watch the pelicans:
they float swanlike, arching their white necks
over only slightly ruffled bundles of wings,
burying awkward beaks in the lake's water.

I clench cold fists in my Marks and Spencer's jacket
and secretly test my accent once again:
St James's Park; St James's Park; St James's Park.

FLEUR ADCOCK (b. 1934)

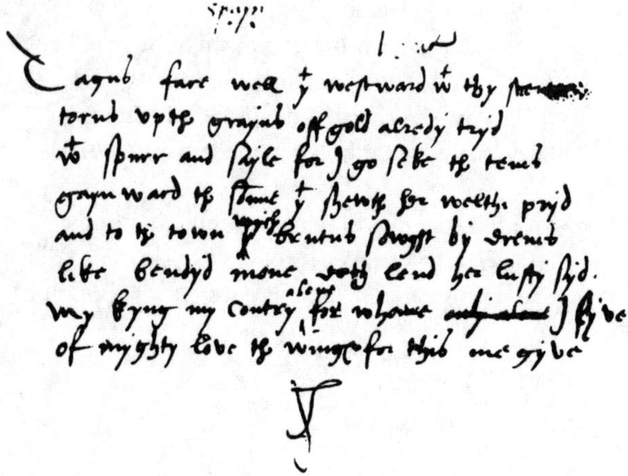
Tagus fare well that westward with thy stremes
torns vp the grayns off gold alredy tryd
with spurr and sayle for I go seke the tems
gaynward the sonne that shewth her welthi pryd
and to the town which brutus sowght by drems
like bendyd mone doth lend her lusty syd.
my kyng my contry alone for whome I lyve
of myghty love the winges for this me gyve

'Tagus farewell' A rare example of a poem in the author's hand, in a handsome leatherbound notebook he kept from 1537 to 1542, which contains over one hundred poems by Wyatt and several by the Earl of Surrey, most of them in the hand of an amanuensis. BL Egerton 2711, f.69. By permission of The British Library Board.

'Tagus farewell'

Tagus farewell, that westward with thy streams
Turns up the grains of gold already tried:
With spur and sail for I go seek the Thames
Gainward the sun that showeth her wealthy pride
And to the town which Brutus sought by dreams
Like bended moon doth lend her lusty side.
My king, my country, alone for whom I live,
Of mighty love the wings for this me give.

SIR THOMAS WYATT (1503–42)

Written in June 1539 in Spain, where Wyatt was Ambassador at the court of Charles V. Wyatt had just been recalled to London by Henry VIII, and the last lines of the poem may reflect some uneasiness at the fate awaiting him at home. The Spanish and Portuguese River Tagus is famous for its gold. Brutus, a descendant of Aeneas, dreamed that he was destined to found a kingdom in Albion.

Prelude I

The winter evening settles down
With smell of steaks in passageways.
Six o'clock.
The burnt-out ends of smoky days.
And now a gusty shower wraps
The grimy scraps
Of withered leaves about your feet
And newspapers from vacant lots;
The showers beat
On broken blinds and chimney-pots,
And at the corner of the street
A lonely cab-horse steams and stamps.

And then the lighting of the lamps.

T. S. ELIOT (1888–1965)

London Airport

Last night in London Airport
I saw a wooden bin
labelled UNWANTED LITERATURE
IS TO BE PLACED HEREIN.
So I wrote a poem
and popped it in.

CHRISTOPHER LOGUE (b. 1926)

Day Trip

Two women, seventies, hold hands
on the edge of Essex,
hair in strong nets,
shrieked laughter echoing gulls
as shingle sucks from under feet
easing in brine.

There must be an unspoken point
when the sea feels like
their future. No longer paddling,
ankles submerge in lace,
in satin ripple.
Dress hems darken.

They do not risk their balance
for the shimmering of ships
at the horizon's sweep
as, thigh deep, they inch on
fingers splayed, wrists bent,
learning to walk again.

CAROLE SATYAMURTI (b. 1939)

'Into my heart an air that kills'

Into my heart an air that kills
  From yon far country blows;
What are those blue remembered hills,
  What spires, what farms are those?

That is the land of lost content,
  I see it shining plain,
The happy highways where I went
  And cannot come again.

from A SHROPSHIRE LAD

A. E. HOUSMAN (1859–1936)

London Bells

Two sticks and an apple,
Ring the bells at Whitechapel.

Old Father Bald Pate,
Ring the bells Aldgate.

Maids in white aprons,
Ring the bells at St. Catherine's.

Oranges and lemons,
Ring the bells at St. Clement's.

When will you pay me?
Ring the bells at the Old Bailey.

When I am rich,
Ring the bells at Fleetditch.

When will that be?
Ring the bells at Stepney.

When I am old,
Ring the great bell at Paul's.

ANON. (early 18th century)

Symphony in Yellow

An omnibus across the bridge
Crawls like a yellow butterfly,
And, here and there, a passer-by
Shows like a little restless midge.

Big barges full of yellow hay
Are moored against the shadowy wharf,
And, like a yellow silken scarf,
The thick fog hangs along the quay.

The yellow leaves begin to fade
And flutter from the Temple elms,
And at my feet the pale green Thames
Lies like a rod of rippled jade.

OSCAR WILDE (1854–1900)

Caricature of Oscar Wilde in a Top Hat. Black and white drawing by Beatrice Whistler. Birnie Philip Bequest. By permission of the Hunterian Art Gallery, University of Glasgow.

To the City of London

London, thou art of towns *A per se*.
   Sovereign of cities, seemliest in sight,
Of high renown, riches, and royalty;
   Of lords, barons, and many a goodly knight;
   Of most delectable lusty ladies bright;
Of famous prelates in habits clerical;
   Of merchants full of substance and might:
London, thou art the flower of cities all.

Gladdeth anon, thou lusty Troy Novaunt,
   City that sometime cleped was New Troy,
In all the earth, imperial as thou standest,
   Princess of towns, of pleasure, and of joy,
   A richer resteth under no Christian roy;
For manly power, with crafts natural,
   Formeth none fairer since the flood of Noy:
London, thou art the flower of cities all.

Gem of all joy, jasper of jocundity,
   Most mighty carbuncle of virtue and valour;
Strong Troy in vigour and in strenuity;
   Of royal cities rose and gilly-flower;
   Empress of towns, exalt in honour;
In beauty bearing the crown imperial;
   Sweet paradise precelling in pleasure:
London, thou art the flower of cities all.

Above all rivers thy river hath renown,
Whose beryl streams, pleasant and preclare,
Under thy lusty walls runneth down;
Where many a swan doth swim with wings fair;
Where many a barge doth sail, and row with oar,
Where many a ship doth rest with top-royal.
O! town of towns, patron and not-compare:
London, thou art the flower of cities all.

Upon thy lusty bridge of pillars white
Be merchants full royal to behold;
Upon thy streets goeth many a seemly knight
In velvet gowns and chains of fine gold.
By Julius Caesar thy Tower founded of old
May be the house of Mars victorial,
Whose artillery with tongue may not be told:
London, thou art the flower of cities all.

Strong be thy walls that about thee stands;
Wise be the people that within thee dwells;
Fresh is thy river with his lusty strands;
Blithe be thy churches, well sounding be thy bells;
Rich be thy merchants in substance that excels;
Fair be thy wives, right lovesome, white and small;
Clear be thy virgins, lusty under kells:
London, thou art the flower of cities all.

Thy famous Mayor, by princely governance,
With sword of justice thee ruleth prudently.
No Lord of Paris, Venice, or Florence
In dignity or honour goeth to him nigh.
He is example, lode-star, and guide;
Principal patron and rose original,
Above all mayors as master most worthy:
London, thou art the flower of cities all.

WILLIAM DUNBAR (1465?–1530?)

The Great Frost

O roving Muse, recall that wondrous year,
When winter reigned in bleak Britannia's air;
When hoary Thames, with frosted osiers crowned,
Was three long moons in icy fetters bound.
The waterman, forlorn along the shore,
Pensive reclines upon his useless oar,
Sees harnessed steeds desert the stony town,
And wander roads unstable, not their own;
Wheels o'er the hardened waters smoothly glide,
And rase with whitened tracks the slippery tide.
Here the fat cook piles high the blazing fire,
And scarce the spit can turn the steer entire.
Booths sudden hide the Thames, long streets appear,
And numerous games proclaim the crowded fair.

from TRIVIA,
OR THE ART OF WALKING THE STREETS OF LONDON

JOHN GAY (1685–1732)

The Embankment

(The Fantasia of a Fallen Gentleman on a Cold, Bitter Night)

Once, in finesse of fiddles found I ecstasy,
In a flash of gold heels on the hard pavement.
Now see I
That warmth's the very stuff of poesy.
Oh, God, make small
The old star-eaten blanket of the sky,
That I may fold it round me and in comfort lie.

T. E. HULME (1883–1917)

Celia Celia

When I am sad and weary
When I think all hope has gone
When I walk along High Holborn
I think of you with nothing on

ADRIAN MITCHELL (b. 1932)

Arrival 1946

The boat docked in at Liverpool.
From the train Tariq stared
at an unbroken line of washing
from the North West to Euston.

These are strange people, he thought –
an Empire, and all this washing,
the underwear, the Englishman's garden.
It was Monday, and very sharp.

MONIZA ALVI (b. 1954)

The Very Leaves of the Acacia-Tree are London

The very leaves of the acacia-tree are London;
London tap-water fills out the fuschia buds in the back garden,
Blackbirds pull London worms out of the sour soil,
The woodlice, centipedes, eat London, the wasps even.
London air through stomata of myriad leaves
And million lungs of London breathes.
Chlorophyll and haemoglobin do what life can
To purify, to return this great explosion
To sanity of leaf and wing.
Gradual and gentle the growth of London Pride,
And sparrows are free of all the time in the world:
Less than a window-pane between.

KATHLEEN RAINE (b. 1908)

from **Summoned by Bells**

Great was my joy with London at my feet –
All London mine, five shillings in my hand
And not expected back till after tea!
Great was our joy, Ronald Hughes Wright's and mine,
To travel by the Underground all day
Between the rush hours, so that very soon
There was no station, north to Finsbury Park,
To Barking eastwards, Clapham Common south,
No temporary platform in the west
Among the Actons and the Ealings, where
We had not once alighted. Metroland
Beckoned us out to lanes in beechy Bucks –
Goldschmidt and Howland (in a wooden hut
Beside the station): 'Most attractive sites
Ripe for development'; Charrington's for coal;
And not far off the neo-Tudor shops.

JOHN BETJEMAN (1906–84)

A 5
ALTUS. Pars 2.
64.
Good sausage
New oysters new, new plaise new new
mackarell new,
Ha' ye any kitchinstuffe mayds.
Ha ye any kitchinstuffe mayds
I ha' ripe cowcumbers ripe
Salt, salt, salt to barge to, Hard onyons hard, Al'a black

The Cries of London

Here's fine rosemary, sage, and thyme.
Come buy my ground ivy.
Here's fetherfew, gilliflowers and rue.
Come buy my knotted marjorum, ho!
Come buy my mint, my fine green mint.
Here's fine lavender for your cloaths.
Here's parsley and winter-savory,
And hearts-ease, which all do choose.
Here's balm and hissop, and cinquefoil,
All fine herbs, it is well known.
  Let none despise the merry, merry cries
  Of famous London-town!

Here's fine herrings, eight a groat.
Hot codlins, pies and tarts.
New mackerel! have to sell.
Come buy my Wellfleet oysters, ho!
Come buy my whitings fine and new.
Wives, shall I mend your husbands horns?
I'll grind your knives to please your wives,
And very nicely cut your corns.
Maids, have you any hair to sell,
Either flaxen, black, or brown?
  Let none despise the merry, merry cries
  Of famous London-town!

ANON. (17th century)

The Cries of London A setting by Orlando Gibbons of several London 'Cries' for five singers and five viol players. BL. Add.MS 29373, f.33v. By permission of The British Library Board.

NOTES TO THE POEMS

17 **'Into my heart an air that kills'** Like *Day Trip*, on p. 16, Housman's poem was composed in London about a place far removed in spirit from city life. Usually read as a lament for the lost innocence of childhood, the short lyric, No. 40 in *A Shropshire Lad*, gains poignancy from the fact that it was drafted when Housman was living in Highgate, travelling daily to his job as a clerk in the Chancery Lane Patent Office.

18 **London Bells** From *Tommy Thumb's Pretty Song Book* (1744), Vol. 2. A later version provides the words for a popular children's game:

> Oranges and lemons
> Say the bells of St. Clement's.
>
> You owe me five farthings,
> Say the bells of St. Martin's.
>
> When will you pay me?
> Say the bells of Old Bailey.
>
> When I grow rich,
> Say the bells of Shoreditch.
>
> When will that be?
> Say the bells of Stepney.
>
> I'm sure I don't know,
> Says the great bell at Bow.
>
> Here comes a candle to light you to bed,
> Here comes a chopper to chop off your head.
>
> *Chop, chop, chop, chop, chop!*

According to Iona and Peter Opie (*The Oxford Dictionary of Nursery Rhymes*), 'The days of public executions have been cited, when the condemned were led along the street to the accompaniment of the tolling of bells.'

20 **To the City of London** The full text of this poem, usually attributed to the Scots poet William Dunbar, is copied into The British Library copy of *The Chronicle of London 1215–1509*, where the poem is said to have been 'made' while the company was sitting at dinner.

ACKNOWLEDGEMENTS

Fleur Adcock: 'Immigrant' from *Selected Poems* (1983). © Fleur Adcock 1983. Reprinted by permission of Oxford University Press.

Moniza Alvi: 'Arrival 1946' from *The Country at my Shoulder* (1993) © Moniza Alvi 1993. Reprinted by permission of Oxford University Press.

John Betjeman: 'Summoned by Bells' © John Betjeman 1960. Reprinted by permission of John Murray.

T. S. Eliot: 'Prelude I' from *Collected Poems 1909–1962* by T. S. Eliot, © T. S. Eliot 1963, 1964. Reprinted by permission of Faber and Faber.

A. E. Housman: 'Into my heart an air that kills' from *A Shropshire Lad.* Reprinted by permission of The Society of Authors as the literary representative of the Estate of A.E. Housman.

Christopher Logue: 'London Airport' from *Ode to the Dodo. Poems 1953–1978* by Christopher Logue, © Christoper Logue 1981. Reprinted by permission of Faber and Faber.

Adrian Mitchell 'Celia, Celia' from *For Beauty Douglas* (Allison & Busby), © Adrian Mitchell 1982. Reprinted by permission of Peters, Fraser & Dunlop; none of Adrian Mitchell's poems is to be used in connection with any examination whatsoever.

Grace Nichols: 'Like a Beacon' from *The Fat Black Woman's Poems* by Grace Nichols, published by Virago Press 1984, © Grace Nichols 1984. Reprinted by permission of Virago Press.

Kathleen Raine: 'The Very Leaves of the Acacia-Tree are London' from *Collected Poems 1935–1980*, © Kathleen Raine. Reprinted by permission of the author.

Carole Satyamurti: 'Day Trip' from *Broken Moon* (1987), © Carole Satyamurti 1987. Reprinted by permission of Oxford University Press.

Ken Smith: 'Encounter at St. Martin's' from *Terra* (1986), © Ken Smith 1986. Reprinted by permission of Bloodaxe Books.

A NOTE OF THANKS

'Poems on the Underground' wish to thank London Underground Ltd, London Arts Board, the British Council and the Stefan Zweig Programme of The British Library.

The posters of poems displayed on the Underground can be purchased from the London Transport Museum, Freepost, Covent Garden, London WC2E 7BB.